Cool SIDES & SALADS

Easy & Fun Comfort Food

ALEX KUSKOWSKI

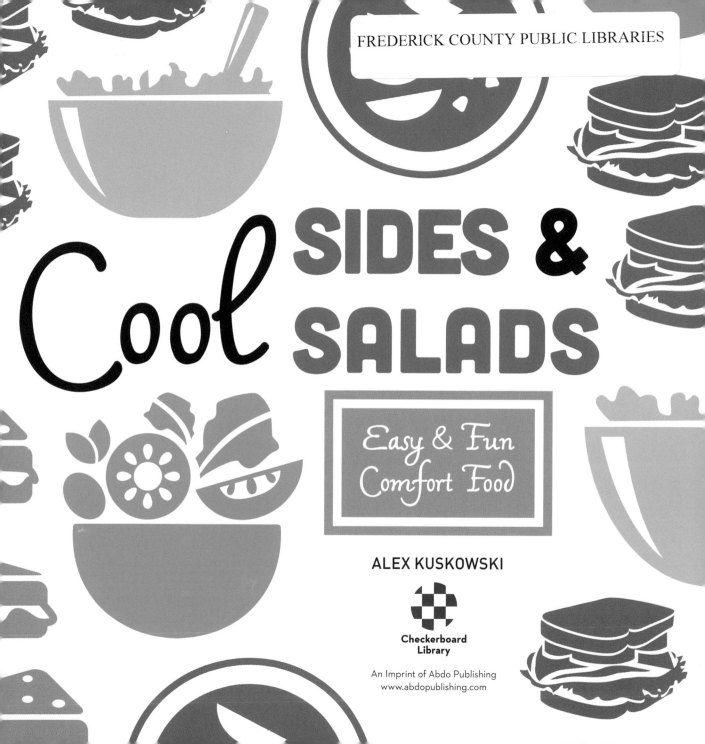

Checkerboard Library

An Imprint of Abdo Publishing
www.abdopublishing.com

www.abdopublishing.com

Published by Abdo Publishing, a division of ABDO, PO Box 398166, Minneapolis, Minnesota 55439. Copyright © 2015 by Abdo Consulting Group, Inc. International copyrights reserved in all countries. No part of this book may be reproduced in any form without written permission from the publisher. Checkerboard Library™ is a trademark and logo of Abdo Publishing.

Printed in the United States of America, North Mankato, Minnesota
102014
012015

Editor: Liz Salzmann
Content Developer: Nancy Tuminelly
Cover and Interior Design and Production:
Colleen Dolphin, Mighty Media, Inc.
Food Production: Frankie Tuminelly
Photo Credits: Colleen Dolphin, Shutterstock

The following manufacturers/names appearing in this book are trademarks: Marukan®, Oster®, Pyrex®, Roundy's®, Thai Kitchen®

Library of Congress Cataloging-in-Publication Data
Kuskowski, Alex.
  Cool sides & salads : easy & fun comfort food / Alex Kuskowski.
    pages cm. -- (Cool home cooking)
  Audience: Ages 7-14.
  Includes index.
  ISBN 978-1-62403-503-6
  1. Salads--Juvenile literature. I. Title. II. Title: Cool sides and salads.
  TX740.K796 2015
  641.83--dc23
                    2014024639

SAFETY FIRST!

Some recipes call for activities or ingredients that require caution. If you see these symbols, ask an adult for help.

HOT STUFF!
This recipe requires the use of a stove or oven. Always use pot holders when handling hot objects.

SUPER SHARP!
This recipe includes the use of a sharp **utensil** such as a knife or grater.

CONTENTS

EXCELLENT EXTRAS!

Any good homemade meal needs **delicious** extras. Make delicious homemade **salads** and side dishes! They make any meal complete. Extra dishes can make or break a meal.

Cooking food at home is healthy and tasty. It can be a lot of fun too. Many canned or frozen foods have extra unhealthy ingredients. With the food you make you know exactly what's in it. It's easy to make a recipe that's **unique** to you. Cook a recipe just the way you like it. Add fresh ingredients to make flavors pop. You can even share what you make with others.

Put the flavor back in your food. Start making home cooked meals! Learn how to serve up some **delectable** extras for your next meal. Check out the recipes in this book.

THE BASICS

Get your cooking started off right with these basic tips!

ASK PERMISSION

Before you cook, ask **permission** to use the kitchen, cooking tools, and ingredients. If you'd like to do something yourself, say so! Just remember to be safe. If you would like help, ask for it! Always get help when you are using a stove or oven.

BE PREPARED

Be organized. Knowing where everything is makes cooking easier and more fun!

Read the directions all the way through before you start. Remember to follow the directions in order.

The most important ingredient in great cooking is preparation! Make sure you have everything you'll need.

Put each ingredient in a separate bowl before starting.

BE SMART, BE SAFE

Always have an adult nearby for hot jobs, such as using the oven or stove.

Have an adult around when using a sharp tool, such as a knife or grater. Always be careful when using them!

Remember to turn pot handles toward the back of the stove. That way you avoid accidentally knocking them over.

BE NEAT, BE CLEAN

Start with clean hands, clean tools, and a clean work surface.

Tie back long hair so it stays out of the food.

Wear comfortable clothing and roll up long sleeves.

COOL COOKING TERMS

HERE ARE SOME HELPFUL TERMS YOU NEED TO KNOW!

CUBE / DICE

Cube and *dice* mean to cut something into small squares.

BEAT

Beat means to mix well using a whisk or electric mixer.

GRATE

Grate means to shred something into small pieces using a grater.

CHOP

Chop means to cut into small pieces.

GREASE

Grease means to coat something with butter, oil, or cooking spray.

PEEL

Peel means to remove the skin, often with a peeler.

STIR

Stir means to mix ingredients together, usually with a large spoon.

ROLL

Roll means to wrap something around itself into a tube.

TOSS

Toss means to turn ingredients over to coat them with seasonings.

SPREAD

Spread means to make a smooth layer with a **utensil**.

WHISK

Whisk means to beat quickly by hand with a whisk or a fork.

COOL TOOLS

HERE ARE SOME OF THE TOOLS YOU WILL NEED!

baking sheet

cutting board

measuring cups

measuring spoons

mixing bowls

mixing spoon

paper towels

peeler

pot holders

saucepan

serving glasses

sharp knife

star cookie cutter

strainer

toaster

toothpicks

whisk

COOL INGREDIENTS

HERE ARE SOME OF THE INGREDIENTS YOU WILL NEED!

avocado

baby lettuce

bacon

blueberries

carrots

cilantro

coconut milk

garlic

ginger

green cabbage

green onions

jalapeño pepper

lemon juice

onion

pea pods

pecans

red bell pepper

red cabbage

red onion

red potatoes

rice paper wrappers

rice vinegar

romaine lettuce

rotisserie chicken

serrano pepper

soy sauce

sweet chili sauce

yellow squash

zucchini

BACON CHEESE MORSELS

Chow down on a tasty snack!

 MAKES 10 SERVINGS

INGREDIENTS

non-stick cooking spray

6 ounces cream cheese

½ cup grated cheddar
   cheese

1 jalapeño pepper,
   chopped

10 slices bread

10 slices bacon,
   cut in half

TOOLS

measuring cups

sharp knife

cutting board

grater

baking sheet

mixing bowl

mixing spoon

toothpicks

pot holders

1 Preheat the oven to 375 degrees. Grease the baking sheet with butter.

2 Put the cream cheese, cheddar cheese, and pepper in a bowl. Stir well.

3 Cut the crusts off the bread slices. Then cut the slices in half. Spread some of the cheese mixture on each half.

4 Lay a bacon slice flat. Put a slice of bread on the bacon with the cheese side up. Line up the end of the bread with the end of the bacon.

5 Roll the bacon and bread together. Keep going until the bacon is wrapped completely around the bread. Put a toothpick through the roll to hold it together. Put the bacon wrap on the baking sheet.

6 Repeat steps 4 and 5 with the rest of the bread and bacon slices.

7 Bake for 25 to 35 minutes, or until the bacon is cooked completely. Remove them from the oven.

2

3

5

SPICY VEGGIE SALAD

A whole new way to get your daily dose of veggies!

 MAKES 4 SERVINGS

INGREDIENTS

2 tablespoons olive oil
1 onion, chopped
3 tablespoons butter
2 garlic cloves, chopped
1 red bell pepper, diced
1 jalapeño, diced
1 zucchini, cubed
1 yellow squash, cubed
½ teaspoon sugar
½ teaspoon salt
½ teaspoon pepper
1 tomato, diced
¼ tablespoon cilantro

TOOLS

sharp knife
cutting board
measuring cups
measuring spoons
large saucepan
mixing spoon
pot holders

1. Put the olive oil, onion, and 1 tablespoon butter in a large saucepan. Cook over medium-low heat for 5 minutes. Stir often.

2. Add the garlic. Cook and stir for 2 minutes.

3. Add the red pepper and jalapeño. Cook and stir for 2 minutes.

4. Add the zucchini and squash. Cook and stir for 5 minutes.

5. Add the sugar, salt, pepper, and remaining butter. Cook and stir for 2 minutes. Stir in the tomatoes and cilantro. Remove from heat. Serve hot.

SUMMER SALAD WRAP

Take your salad to go!

 MAKES 6 SERVINGS

INGREDIENTS

¼ cup mayonnaise

1 tablespoon mustard

1 tablespoon lemon juice

1 teaspoon paprika

4 8-inch (20 cm) rice paper wrappers

10 large lettuce leaves

5 carrots, sliced into strips

1 tomato, chopped

¼ cup grated cheddar cheese

TOOLS

measuring cups

measuring spoons

sharp knife

cutting board

grater

mixing bowls

whisk

1 Make the dressing. In a small mixing bowl, whisk together the mayonnaise, mustard, lemon juice, and paprika.

2 Fill a mixing bowl with warm water. Soak a rice paper wrapper in the water for about 10 seconds. Take it out when it softens. Lay the wrapper flat on a cutting board.

3 Lay a lettuce leaf on the wrapper. Put some of the carrot strips, tomato, and cheese on the lettuce. Top with 1 tablespoon of dressing.

4 Fold the bottom of the wrapper up. Fold the top of the wrapper down.

5 Starting at one side, roll up the wrapper with all the ingredients inside.

6 Repeat steps 2 through 5 to make more **salad** wraps.

3

4

5

MINI POTATO BITES

These potato bites will hit the spot!

  MAKES 6 SERVINGS

INGREDIENTS

non-stick cooking spray
15 red potatoes
1 tablespoon olive oil
1 teaspoon salt
1 teaspoon pepper
4 ounces cream cheese
1 garlic clove, chopped
2 tablespoons
  sour cream
2 tablespoons chopped
  chives

TOOLS

sharp knife
cutting board
measuring cups
measuring spoons
baking sheet
mixing bowls
mixing spoon
spoon
pot holders

1 Preheat the oven to 450. Grease the baking sheet with cooking spray.

2 Cut the potatoes in half **lengthwise**. Put them in a mixing bowl. Add the olive oil, salt, and pepper. Stir until the potatoes are coated. Put the potatoes on the baking sheet cut side up. Bake 30 minutes. Let the potatoes cool.

3 Scoop a teaspoon of potato out of the middle of each potato. Put the teaspoons of potato in a mixing bowl.

4 Add the cream cheese, garlic, and sour cream. Stir well.

5 Fill the holes in the potatoes with the potato and cream cheese mixture. Put the potatoes back in the oven for 15 minutes. Take them out of the oven. Sprinkle the chives on top.

TIP
Cut a small slice off the bottom of the potatoes to keep them from rocking on the baking sheet.

CHICKEN AVOCADO SALAD

Try this tasty, tart salad!

 MAKES 5 SERVINGS

INGREDIENTS

1 can black beans

2 tablespoons olive oil

3 tablespoons mayonnaise

1 teaspoon cumin

2 teaspoons chopped serrano pepper

3 tablespoons lime juice

½ cup chopped grilled or roasted chicken

½ cup chopped romaine lettuce

½ cup chopped green onion

½ cup tomatoes

½ cup corn kernels

½ cup chopped fresh cilantro

1 large avocado, peeled and diced

TOOLS

measuring cups

measuring spoons

sharp knife

cutting board

peeler

strainer

mixing bowls

whisk

mixing spoon

1 Rinse the black beans. Drain them well.

2 In a large mixing bowl, whisk together the olive oil, mayonnaise, cumin, serrano pepper, and 2 tablespoons lime juice. Stir in the beans. Let the mixture sit for 5 minutes.

3 Add the chicken, lettuce, green onion, tomatoes, corn and cilantro. Stir well.

4 Put the avocado and 1 tablespoon lime juice in a small mixing bowl. Stir to coat the avocado with lime juice. Add the avocado to the **salad**.

TIP

Serve this salad inside pita bread for a tasty **sandwich**!

SURPRISE THAI SALAD

Combine cuisines with this tasty salad!

  MAKES 4 SERVINGS

INGREDIENTS

DRESSING

½ cup sweet chili sauce

¼ cup rice vinegar

¼ cup coconut milk

3 tablespoons brown sugar

2 garlic cloves, chopped

3 green onions, sliced

1 tablespoon ginger, grated

1 tablespoon lime juice

1 tablespoon soy sauce

SALAD

1 red cabbage, chopped

1 green cabbage, chopped

2 cups chopped red pepper

½ cup chopped red onion

½ cup chopped carrots

½ cup pea pods

½ cup cilantro

⅔ cup peanuts, chopped

TOOLS

measuring cups

measuring spoons

sharp knife

cutting board

saucepan

whisk

mixing bowl

mixing spoon

4 salad bowls

pot holders

1. Whisk the dressing ingredients together in a saucepan. Cook over medium-low heat for 5 minutes. Remove from heat.

2. Put the red cabbage, green cabbage, red pepper, onion, carrots, pea pods, and cilantro in a mixing bowl. Toss to combine the ingredients.

3. Divide the **salad** between the salad bowls. Top each salad with peanuts.

4. Pour dressing on each salad. Serve right away.

STARRY B.L.T. BITES

Serve up delicious mini sandwiches!

 MAKES 6 SERVINGS

INGREDIENTS

6 slices bacon

6 slices bread

2 small tomatoes, sliced

2 lettuce leaves

4 tablespoons mayonnaise

1 teaspoon salt

1 teaspoon pepper

TOOLS

sharp knife

cutting board

measuring spoons

frying pan

paper towels

toaster

star cookie cutter

dinner knife

toothpicks

pot holders

1 Cook the bacon in the frying pan for 5 to 10 minutes or until it is **crispy**. Lay the bacon on paper towels to drain. Cut the bacon slices in half.

2 Toast all of the bread. Use the cookie cutter to cut two stars out of each slice. Spread mayonnaise on one side of each slice.

3 Tear the lettuce into six pieces about the size of the cookie cutter.

4 Put a piece of lettuce on six of the bread stars. Put two pieces of bacon on top of the lettuce. Put a tomato slice on top of the bacon.

5 Top each **sandwich** with another bread star. Stick a toothpick in the middle of each sandwich.

FUN FRUIT SALAD

Serve this sweet salad to friends or family!

 MAKES 6 SERVINGS

INGREDIENTS

1 cup vanilla yogurt

8 ounces cream cheese

½ cup white sugar

1 teaspoon vanilla extract

1 cup green grapes

1 cup red grapes

⅓ cup strawberries

½ cup blueberries

2 tablespoons brown sugar

1 cup chopped pecans

TOOLS

measuring cups

measuring spoons

sharp knife

cutting board

paper towels

mixing bowls

electric mixer

serving glasses

1. Put the yogurt, cream cheese, white sugar, and vanilla extract in a large mixing bowl. Beat with an electric mixer. Refrigerate 1 hour.

2. Wash the grapes, strawberries, and blueberries. Pat them dry with a paper towel. Chop the strawberries.

3. Put a layer of fruit in the bottom of a serving cup. Add a layer of the yogurt mixture. Alternate fruit and yogurt layers until the cup is full.

4. Top with brown sugar and pecans.

5. Repeat steps 3 and 4 to fill the other serving glasses.

CONCLUSION

This book has some seriously **delicious** side dish and **salad** recipes! But don't stop there. Get creative. Add your favorite ingredients to the recipes. Cook it your way.

Check out other types of home cooking. Make tasty breads, main dishes, drinks, soups, and even **desserts**. Put together a meal everyone will cheer for.

WEBSITES

To learn more about Cool Home Cooking, visit booklinks.abdopublishing.com. These links are routinely monitored and updated to provide the most current information available.

GLOSSARY

crispy – hard, thin, and easy to break.

delectable – very pleasing or delightful.

delicious – very pleasing to taste or smell.

dessert – a sweet food, such as fruit, ice cream, or pastry, served after a meal.

lengthwise – in the direction of the longest side.

permission – when a person in charge says it's okay to do something.

salad – a mixture of raw vegetables usually served with a dressing.

sandwich – two pieces of bread with a filling, such as meat, cheese, or peanut butter, between them.

unique – different, unusual, or special.

utensil – a tool used to prepare or eat food.

INDEX